RHS

Inspiring every

STICKS, STARS, DENS & STONES

FUN DAYS IN THE GREAT OUTDOORS

THIS BOOK BELONGS TO

....

CONTENTS

LET'S GO EXPLORING

There's never a bad time to explore nature. All through the year there are fascinating and beautiful things to discover in gardens, woodlands, rivers and along the coast – and whether it's on your doorstep, or further afield, there's always something fun to do and something new to see.

Come with us on an adventure trail through the dazzling variety of the natural world, and meet the animals, plants and habitats that flourish all around us. Along the way we'll find out how to track animals, navigate by the stars and build a bee hotel, as well as much, much more.

Let's go!

STAY SAFE

Taking risks and overcoming challenges are important parts of being an outdoor adventurer, but it's even more important to look after yourself! Follow these safety tips when you're out and about.

Look After Yourself

Make sure you're with a grown-up whenever you go exploring in nature. Take extra care when exploring around water and keep an eye on younger brothers and sisters.

Wash your hands after going outside – this is especially important if you have touched soil or stagnant water. Use soap and warm water, and scrub for at least twenty seconds.

Only use sharp tools like scissors if you have been given permission by a grown-up and know how to use them safely. If an activity requires a knife, make sure there is a grown-up there to help.

**Look out for more safety
tips throughout the book.**

Drink plenty of water, particularly if it's a hot day, even if you don't feel thirsty. Wear a sun hat and sun cream to avoid getting a sunburn or getting heatstroke.

Respect nature and never harm any living creature or plants. Certain insects, such as some bees and wasps, have stings, and a few caterpillars have hairs that can cause a rash. Do not touch or swat at these insects.

Look After Nature

Always leave wild areas exactly as you found them. Keep an eye out for wildlife homes, such as nests and burrows, and be particularly careful around them.

Make sure you have permission to pick flowers or other plants in an area before you do so, and only take a little so as not to damage the plant. Take all your belongings and litter home.

WOODLAND TRAIL

Trees provide shelter, food, and a home to all kinds of things. Here are some unique woodlands to keep an eye out for.

Ancient Woodlands
For centuries, humans have relied on woods for food, fuel and shelter. These woodlands have seen constant tree cover for at least several hundred years, while they might have been pollarded (a tree's upper branches are cut) and coppiced (trees cut down to allow new growth). They have developed a unique mixture of plants, animals, fungi, insects and even bacteria that can't be found anywhere else in the world.

Forest
Large areas thickly covered by trees, undergrowth and other habitats, such as heathland, are called forests. Forests often have coniferous trees (evergreen trees that have needle-like leaves) such as pine, spruce, juniper and yew – and are home to animals, such as deer and pine martens.

Broadleaved Woodlands
Many broadleaved woodlands have deciduous trees, such as oak, ash, beech and birch that lose their leaves in the winter. They are home to animals, such as hedgehogs, badgers and bats.

Urban Woodlands
Made up of trees that grow well in towns or cities and are resistant to pollution, such as plane, birch or horse chestnut, urban woodlands help animals, such as foxes, birds and squirrels, thrive.

Did you know?
Earth has more than
three trillion trees – that's
billions more than there
are stars in our galaxy!

WOODLAND TREES

There are more than 50,000 different species of tree – more than you can shake a stick at! Here are some distinctive and beautiful trees from around the world.

European Larch

Growing across Europe, the European larch is a type of coniferous tree, but unlike other coniferous trees, it is also deciduous. Its needles change from a vivid green to a golden yellow, before dropping in autumn.

Did you know?

Some of the biggest and oldest living things on Earth are trees. Some giant redwood can grow more than a hundred metres tall, and one bristlecone pine is thought to be more than 5,000 years old.

Hornbeam

"Hornbeam" means "hard tree", and the wood from the hornbeam is one of the strongest in the world. Native to the UK, hornbeams can be identifed by their many branches and greenish hanging flowers called "catkins".

Acacia

Acacias grow in dry, hot places, such as Australia, Africa, Asia and the USA. Many kinds of acacia have sharp thorns which have a bitter taste to stop animals from eating them.

Baobab

Native to Africa, baobabs are known as "upside-down trees", because their branches look like tree roots. The huge trunks often become hollow inside as the tree grows – some are big enough for many people to shelter inside.

Juniper

Found in the UK and Europe, junipers are evergreen trees – they keep their needles all year round. Many bird species like to nest in junipers as the branches are very dense and give good cover.

Persian Silk

In the Persian language this tree is named "*shabkhosb*", meaning "sleeping tree". Native to Asia and Africa, the Persian silk tree is most likely named after its silky flowers.

IDENTIFYING TREES

There are all kinds of ways to identify the many different kinds of trees that grow in our wild and urban spaces – here are a few different things to look out for.

Leaves and Needles

Trees can have leaves, needles or scales. They use these to capture sunlight, which they use to make sugars to feed on so they can grow.

Broadleaf trees have "simple" or "compound" leaves. Apple and plane trees have simple leaves, where a single leaf is attached to a single stem. Ash and horse chestnut trees have compound leaves with several "leaflets" attached to a single stem.

Horse Chestnut   **Apple**   **Plane**   **Ash**

Trees such as pines, yews or larches have needles, and you may be able to tell them apart by how the needles are arranged. Cypresses have scales – flat and shield-shaped – overlapping on the shoots.

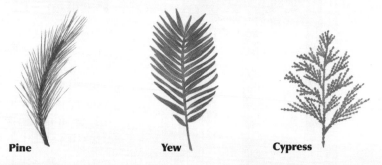

Pine   **Yew**   **Cypress**

Fruits and Seed Pods

Most plants grow from seeds. Trees are rooted to the spot and can't move to spread their seeds, so they have developed other ways to help their seeds travel.

Some fruits, such as apples, contain seeds. Their flesh protects the seeds and attracts animals who feed on them – once the fruit is eaten the animals may throw away the seeds, bury them for later or simply poop them out!

Apple   **Sycamore**   **Pine Cone**

Sycamore seeds are called "helicopter seeds" because they spin in the air when they fall from the tree. Pine trees make woody "fruit". The hard cones keep the seeds safe until they are ready to be released.

Bark

Not all tree bark looks the same. It comes in a wide variety of colours, and has all sorts of different patterns and textures. Beech tree bark is smooth and grey, while Scots pine is orange-brown and broken into what looks like crinkly plates or scales.

Oak   **Beech**   **Scots Pine**

As trees get older the patterns of grooves and bumps on their bark will become deeper and craggier. Old aspen trees will show diamond-shaped pits called lenticels; while the lenticels on cherry trees are horizontal and often peel off as the tree gets older.

Cherry Tree   **Silver Birch**   **Aspen**

SPOTTING THE SIGNS

Woodlands are home to all sorts of animals, and you can see the signs everywhere, whether it's their tracks (footprints), the remains of their meals, or – yes – their poo!

Bank Vole

Very fast on their feet, bank voles travel through undergrowth, live in shallow burrows and use their big ears to listen for predators. You might spot them in hedgerows or on the edge of woodlands.

Hare

Much like rabbits but bigger with long, black-tipped ears, which you might spot poking up from long grass. A hare's hind paws are bigger and longer than its front paws, which makes hare tracks easy to recognize.

Badger

These creatures live in underground burrows and tunnels called setts. Badgers dig these using their powerful claws, and sleep there during the daytime.

ANIMAL HOMES

Nature is full of fascinating wildlife, and each animal species have distinct homes to suit their specific needs – if you keep an eye out you may spot some!

Rabbit Warren

Rabbits live in groups of up to 30 rabbits. Females usually create their homes by digging complex tunnels underground, called warrens. The tunnels can also be used to escape from any predators.

Bat Roost

Bats are nocturnal, which means they are most active at night-time. They roost (sleep) in hollow trees, roofs and caves during daytime. They hang upside down, with their wings wrapped around their bodies, ready to take off if disturbed.

Owl Nest

Some owl species like to nest in tree hollows, a partially open hole, which has naturally formed in a tree trunk. After making their nests there, the owls lay eggs and raise their young.

WOODLANDS CHECKLIST

Plants and fungi provide food for all kinds of creatures. Here are some of the tasty – and not so tasty – foods that you might find in woodlands, and who likes to eat them. Can you spot any of these foods or the animals that like to eat them on your woodlands adventure?

Fruit

- ☐ badgers
- ☐ bank voles
- ☐ mice

Berries

- ☐ birds
- ☐ red deer
- ☐ foxes

Nuts

- ☐ squirrels
- ☐ nut weevils
- ☐ dormice

Seeds

- ☐ badgers
- ☐ wood mice
- ☐ squirrels

Fungi

- [ ] fungus beetles
- [ ] worms
- [ ] slugs

Tree Bark

- [ ] sika deer
- [ ] voles
- [ ] bark beetles

Grass

- [ ] deer
- [ ] grasshoppers
- [ ] rabbits

Leaves

- [ ] beavers
- [ ] slugs
- [ ] caterpillars

SETTLE IN FOR THE NIGHT

Choosing the right campsite is the difference between a good night's sleep and an uncomfortable or even disastrous one. Here are some tips and tricks for camping safely and happily.

Make sure you're allowed to camp in the site you've chosen! Find a wide, flat open area. Get rid of any rocks, branches or anything else you wouldn't want to sleep on. If there are pine trees nearby, you can spread a layer of pine needles to make the ground softer under your tent.

Avoid pitching your tent in a dip or hollow in the ground. If it rains, water will run down and pool under your tent, which is no fun at all.

Don't pitch your tent directly under trees – in high winds this could lead to branches falling on you.

Place the tent opening away from the wind, and try to find a spot where your tent is sheltered from it, as it will tug at your tent pegs and try to blow you away.

Pitching your tent so that it will be in the shade when the sun rises will help prevent overheating in the morning.

BUILDING A DEN

What will your den be? A secret hideaway or a fairy grotto? Let your imagination run wild in the woods. Here are some tips and tricks to build the best den ever!

You will need:

- branches
- rope
- bendy twigs
- mud
- dried leaves

1. You can build a den in your garden or in some woodland – make sure to ask permission first. Pick somewhere open and flat or find a tree with low branches that can support your den.

2. Look for some long, strong branches – these will make the frame for your den. Don't break off any living branches from a tree – instead collect those that have already fallen to the forest floor.

3. When you have about ten large branches stand them up in a triangle shape. Use some rope to tie the tops of the branches together – make sure to ask an adult to help as this can be tricky!

4. Weave some bendy twigs in between the branches to make some walls – be sure to leave room for a door! Layer mud and leaves on your den to help it blend into the woodland.

5. Now your den is built, crawl inside and relax. Use this book to help you observe the nature around you! When you leave, remember to dismantle your den and take your rope home.

WOODLAND SCAVENGER HUNT

Turn your woodland walk into a game by doing a scavenger hunt – and challenge your friends and family to beat your score. Just tick each item off the list whenever you come across one in the woods.

☐ **rabbit**

☐ **spider's web**

☐ **bird's nest**

☐ **wildflowers – pink, red, yellow and white**

☐ **caterpillar**

☐ **animal tracks**

☐ **litter**

☐ **moss growing on a log**

☐ **deer**

☐ **blossom**

25

RIVER TRAIL

When snow or rain falls on hills and mountains, it runs all the way down and back to the sea. The water forms streams as it follows the cracks and folds of the land to flow downhill. The streams join together to form rivers, which run all the way to an ocean, sea or lake.

Rivers are changing all the time. When the temperature is too hot, it can cause water to evaporate faster than it usually would, causing water levels in rivers to drop drastically. In hot countries, if there is a lack of rainfall for a long period of time it can cause a drought, an extended dry period in the normal climate cycle which can last between a few weeks or up to several years.

Rivers can be very deep and wide: the Amazon river in South America is up to 40 kilometres wide, while Africa's Congo river is 220 metres deep, or more – nobody knows for sure!

Rivers are important habitats for all sorts of animals and plants – fish, of course, but also insects, otters, water birds, water voles, frogs and reptiles.

Did you know?
The Nile in North Africa is
the world's longest river. It
stretches an incredible
6,695 km, and flows through
eleven different countries!

PLANTS BY THE RIVER

Different habitats allow different plants to thrive. Look out for these distinctive plants when you're out and about by the river.

Duckweed

The "carpet" of tiny leaves floating on slow-moving rivers is made up of duckweed – each leaf is a single duckweed plant. A mat of duckweed can double in size in just a few days!

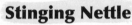

Stinging Nettle

Tiny hairs on the stem and underside of nettle leaves will sting you if you touch them – this helps protect it from being eaten by predators.

Water Forget-Me-Not

This plant grows anywhere that is damp – in shallow waters or on riverbanks. In the summer it produces clusters of sky-blue flowers with five petals and yellow centres.

Comfrey

Found on many riverbanks, comfrey has drooping, bell-shaped flowers, which may be white or pinky-purple. Comfrey grows quickly, flowering from late spring to summer.

Butterbur

People used to wrap their butters in the leaves of this plant, which is how it got its name! It grows tiny, pale pink flowers that are fed on by bees.

RIVER ANIMALS

Here are some of the creatures you might find in or around rivers, streams and ponds.

Kingfisher

When kingfishers are ready to nest and lay eggs they dig tunnels into sandy riverbanks, with a dip at the end of the tunnel so their eggs don't roll out.

Heron

Standing still in shallow ponds and lakes, or slowly pacing at the water's edge, herons wait for fish to swim by, so they can snap them up with their strong bills.

Minnow

Minnows swim in large groups called shoals. When a predator – such as a bigger fish – is near, minnows release a smell to warn each other of danger.

European Otter

An otter's webbed feet and the ability to close its ears and nose lets it dive underwater when looking for food – mainly fish, as well as frogs, crabs and water birds.

Frog

Frogs are patient hunters, letting their food – insects, mainly – come to them. When their prey is close enough, they dart out their long, sticky tongues to grab it and swallow it in one gulp!

Beaver

Beavers construct dams to create still, deep ponds where they can safely build homes called lodges. The homes even have chimneys to help regulate the temperature!

31

EXPLORING RIVERS

It's important to stay safe when exploring near the water. Rivers and canals can be cold, deep and fast-moving, and that means they can be very dangerous. Here are some tips to keep you safe:

1. Never go near water alone. Always have an adult with you, so there is someone to help if you get into trouble.

2. Wear sturdy shoes or boots that have non-slip soles. Look out for signs or flags that may warn you of danger in the area, and pay attention to what they say.

3. Don't drink or swallow river or canal water – it may make you ill – and wash your hands after touching anything you find.

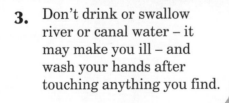

4. Make sure to stay in a group when near water, and don't wander off alone.

5. Be careful near the edge – don't run, and remember that riverbanks can be slippery and crumbly.

6. Remember that rivers and canals can contain sharp rocks, glass and rubbish like tin cans but you might not be able to see them.

7. Throw a leaf into the river or canal to judge how fast the water is flowing, or to find fast-moving currents, but do not get in the water yourself.

33

MAKE A RIVER MAP

Get to know a river, and the animals and plants that live there, by making a map and tracking the ways the different habitats change with the seasons.

Map Key:

- 📍 path
- ⌐ bench
- 🌳 forest
- 🌷 flowers
- 💧 water
- 🌾 willow trees
- 🗻 bushes

0   100   200   300   400   500   600 METRES

You will need:

- graph paper
- ruler
- coloured pencils
- pens
- compass
- calculator

How to make a river map:

1. Map a section of river. Measure the area by counting how many steps it takes to walk along it.

2. Pick a scale for your map. Choose how many metres a square counts as – each 1 cm square could count as 10 m of river. Write the scale in the corner of the map.

3. Sketch the river, show how it curves, widens or narrows from one end of the map to the other. Add in any major features like bridges along the way.

4. Mark any trees, plants or animals you see. Use lots of colours to shade in each area of the river, or use different symbols for each tree species.

5. Add a map key to explain any symbols you use, and a compass rose showing which way is north.

THE WATER CYCLE

Water is constantly moving around our planet – from the surface of the Earth into the air, from clouds back down to Earth, from mountains to rivers and from rivers to the sea. Then it moves around all over again – this is known as the water cycle.

1. Evaporation

The Sun heats up water on the Earth's surface. It evaporates into water vapour (a gas) and rises into the atmosphere.

4. Surface Runoff

Water flows downhill from high ground, forming streams and rivers that flow into the sea. Then the whole cycle begins again.

Did you know?

Some water seeps into cracked or porous rock and forms underground springs, which slowly reach the sea, this in known as "infiltration".

2. Condensation

The water vapour cools back into a liquid and "condenses" to form clouds. The clouds are blown around the world.

3. Precipitation

When the clouds become too heavy with water, it falls back to Earth as precipitation – rain, snow, sleet or hail.

Did you know?

Water also evaporates from plants and trees through their leaves. This is known as "transpiration".

HOW TO MAKE S'MORES

S'mores are sandwiches made of biscuits, chocolate and toasted marshmallow, which are traditionally eaten around the campfire in the United States and Canada.

You will need:

- biscuits, such as digestive or rich tea biscuits
- marshmallows
- chocolate or chocolate spread
- wooden skewers or clean twigs

How to cook on a campfire or barbeque:

1. Put a piece of chocolate or chocolate spread on a biscuit. Ask an adult for help with toasting the marshmallows.

2. Spike a marshmallow on the end of your skewer or twig.

3. Hold the skewer over the fire or hot coals, turning it so that the marshmallow toasts evenly.

4. Squeeze the toasted marshmallow between two biscuits and pull out the skewer. Allow to cool a little before eating.

How to cook in an oven or microwave:

1. Place chocolate on a biscuit, and top with a marshmallow.

2. Place on a baking tray in a preheated oven at 180 °C for 5 minutes, or in a microwave for 15–20 seconds.

3. Remove from the oven or microwave, add a second biscuit on top and squeeze together. And enjoy!

Safety tip: allow your s'more to cool a little before you touch it.

Safety tip: don't forget to keep turning your marshmallow, otherwise it might fall into the fire.

SKIPPING STONES

Skipping, or skimming, stones across water takes a little practice, but once you've got the knack you can have hours of fun challenging your friends and family to beat your score!

You will need:

- a fairly calm body of water, such as a pond, lake or canal
- several smooth, flat stones

Saftey tip: always be careful near the water and make sure to stay with an adult.

Picking a Stone

The idea is to throw the stone so that it strikes the water and skips off the surface, rather than sinking. For that you want a stone that is smooth and flat. Pick a stone that is not too heavy and fits nicely between your thumb and index finger.

Skipping a Stone

Hold the stone so that your thumb and fingers make a "c" shape or a reversed "c" if you're right-handed. Bend your hands back a little and then flick it forward to release the stone, aiming low and straight. The stone needs to be travelling fast, spinning, and with its flat side facing down as it hits the water.

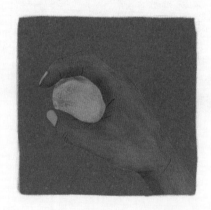

Did you know?
The world record distance for skipping a stone is 121.8 m!

41

MORE RIVERSIDE PLANTS

Each habitat suits different plants – some plants are even unique to that habitat and can't be found anywhere else!

Lesser Celandine

Appearing early in springtime, people used to believe that lesser celandine could predict the weather because they close their petals before rainfall begins.

Yellow Water Lily

While the leaves – or "lily pads" – and yellow cup-shaped flowers float on the surface, the plant's roots can be in the muddy riverbed more than 3 metres down!

Alder Tree

A young alder's leaves and twigs produce a gummy substance that helps keep insects from nibbling them.

White Willow

Willow trees are large, with long leaves that have a layer of silky white hairs on their undersides. They love wet soil and can be found near rivers and lakes.

RIVER SCAVENGER HUNT

It's time to take our scavenger hunt out to the river! See how many of these items you can check off your list:

☐ **boat**

☐ **lily pad**

☐ **swan**

☐ **moorhen**

☐ **minnow**

☐ otter

☐ kingfisher

☐ snail

☐ frog

☐ duck

45

SEASIDE TRAIL

Two thirds of planet Earth is covered in sea water. But what we think of as the separate oceans and seas are just names for different parts of one single enormous ocean. We have five oceans: the Arctic and Southern oceans, near the North and South Poles; the Pacific, the Atlantic and the Indian oceans.

The ocean contains almost all the water in the world. A huge range of creatures live there, from microscopic animals to giant whales. It is so deep in places that no light reaches the ocean's floor, and the weight of water above means that only a few animals can live there without being squashed by it.

The ocean is always moving. You might have seen waves breaking on the coast, and if you stay for a few hours you can watch the sea getting closer to, or drawing away from, the shore: the tide coming in and going out.

Waves on the surface are caused by the wind blowing across the top of the water. The tides are caused by the force of gravity pulling between Earth and the Moon and the Sun.

The ocean is important to life on our planet, but it is fragile. When visiting the seaside, be careful not to disturb the wildlife and take away all your litter so that it doesn't wash into the sea and harm sea life or pollute the water.

Did you know?
The Mariana Trench in the Western Pacific ocean is the deepest known area of the Earth's oceans. It's deepest point measures 11 km (7 miles)!

SEASIDE PLANTS

Plants that grow near the coast need to be happy in sandy, dry soils, and be tough enough to stand up to strong, often salty, winds. The kinds of plants you'll see at the seaside will often be very different to anywhere else!

Pine Tree

Unlike many tree species, pine trees are able to grow in sandy soil, and are strong enough to stand up to storms and the strong winds that blow in from the sea.

Sea Kale

From the same family as cabbage, sea kale has blue-green leaves and clusters of sweet-smelling white flowers. It is often found growing on beaches, as it is able to survive in the salty soil.

Common Gorse

Often found growing on cliffs and rocky places, coomon gorse's dense needle-like leaves and yellow flowers give birds, as well as insects, a place to shelter.

Thrift

Growing in dense mats or cushions of needle-shaped green leaves, thrift has pink flowers in spring and summer. Bees and butterflies often feed on the flowers.

ANIMALS AT THE SEASIDE

Our coasts and oceans are teeming with life, from tiny plankton that you can only see with a microscope, all the way to huge basking sharks and whales.

Bottlenose Dolphin

Dolphins make clicking noises to hunt fish. The noise travels through the water, if it hits something it bounces back as an echo, letting the dolphin know what's there and where to go.

Spotted Cowrie

There are many kinds of cowries, but all have shiny, ridged shells, which are difficult to grip on to – letting these underwater snails slip away from predators.

Cuckoo Wrasse

Male and female cuckoo wrasses look quite different to each other. Males have orange bodies with wavy blue markings. Females are usually smaller with orangey-pink coloured bodies and black and white spots on their backs.

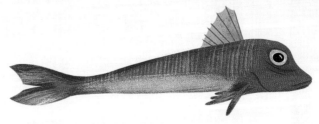

Red Gurnard

Red gurnards are able to separate the lower three spines of their pectoral (chest) fins to search the seabed for food – often looking like they are walking on the sea floor.

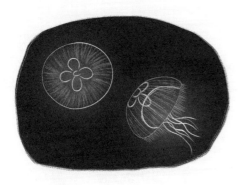

Moon Jelly

Jellyfish have been around for millions of years and are found in seas all over the world. Their bodies are made of ninety-five per cent water – with no brain, blood or heart!

Basking Shark

Despite being the second biggest fish in the sea, basking sharks only eat tiny creatures called zooplankton. They swim with their huge mouths open letting zooplankton float in, and only close their mouths to swallow their food.

51

GO ROCK POOLING

When the tide goes out at the coast a whole world of fascinating creatures is revealed in the rocky pools left behind. Let's see what we can find!

Before you go:

- Look for sheltered, rocky shores, with sandy or pebbly beaches.

- Check a tide table before you go. You will need to know when to turn up for low tide.

- Be certain that you know when the tide will be coming back in.

- Make sure you have sturdy footwear for slippery rocks, the right clothes for the weather, and don't forget to wear sunscreen.

Here are some of the animals you might find:

- [ ] starfish
- [ ] blenny
- [ ] sand eel
- [ ] limpet
- [ ] crab
- [ ] beadlet anemone

1. Find a rock pool. Try not to cast a shadow over it, as this may scare away the animals inside.

2. Dip a bucket or a container into the pool and bring it back up. What have you found?

3. After you've had a close look, carefully release the animals back into the rock pool.

Safety tip: take an adult with you when rock pooling, and always wash your hands afterwards.

MAKE YOUR OWN FOSSIL

Ammonites were prehistoric sea creatures who lived at the same time as the dinosaurs. They had a spiral shell, which is sometimes preserved as a fossil. You can find ammonite fossils on beaches when the tide is going out, preserved in sedimentary rocks, such as limestone or sandstone – keep a sharp eye out to find them! You can even make your own ammonite "fossils".

You will need:

- 250g plain flour
- 125g salt
- 125ml water
- string
- a baking tray
- vegetable oil
- baking paper

1. Mix the flour and salt in a bowl. Gradually add the water, working it together into a ball of dough.

2. Roll the dough out like a long sausage. It should be thicker at one end and thinner at the other.

3. Loop some string around the dough. The ridges will make your fossil look like a real ammonite!

Safety tip: always take an adult with you if you're going fossil hunting, and be very careful near cliffs.

4. Starting with the thinner end, roll the sausage into the shape of an ammonite.

5. Add features, such as a spine, to your ammonite fossil by pinching the dough.

6. Put your "fossil" on a paper-lined baking tray and bake at 120°C for three hours.

Ask an adult for help when using an oven.

7. Once it's completely cooled you could bury your "fossil" in the garden and go fossil hunting!

HOW TO MAKE SAND SCULPTURES

Anyone who has been to the beach will have made a sandcastle or two. You simply fill a bucket with wet sand, turn it over onto the beach, and carefully pull the bucket away. You can also use this method to make a block of sand to carve into shape

1. Wet sand is heavy and make it hard to flip the bucket over. So, it's a good idea to cut the bottom off a bucket (ask an adult to do this for you). Lay it on the beach, and pack sand into it through the opening.

2. Pack in the wet sand as tightly as you can, then tap the sides of the bucket with a stick to free it a little from the sand block. You should be able to gently lift the bucket away.

3. Use a spatula, potato peeler or even a spoon to carve the sand into any shape you want. Use a paper straw to blow little bits of shaved-away sand off your sculpture.

4. As you sculpt, the sand will start to dry and fall apart. If you want more time to work on it, try misting it with seawater from a spray bottle. What will you sculpt?

Grab your bucket and spade – and maybe a few other bits and bobs – and make some sand sculptures!

57

SHELL SCAVENGER HUNT

A trip to the seaside is a great opportunity to go on a shell scavenger hunt. Many creatures – such as sea snails, clams and oysters – grow hard shells to protect themselves from predators who might want to eat them. Hermit crabs even move from one abandoned shell to another as they grow larger! How many of these can you find?

☐ Whelk

Whelks (a kind of sea snail) are one of the most common shells at the seaside.

Once you've spotted the shells be sure to put them back where you found them, as some seaside animals rely on them to survive.

☐ Mussel

A mollusc that lives inside a hinged blue-grey shell, longer than it is wide.

☐ Thin Tellin

A small mollusc with flat, rosy-pink or yellow triangular shells.

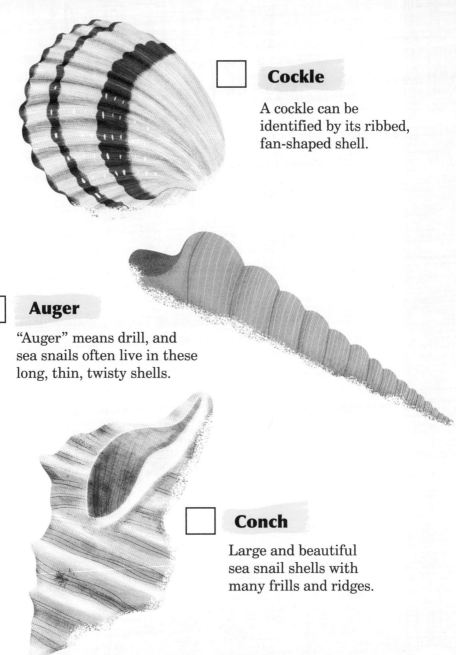

Cockle

A cockle can be identified by its ribbed, fan-shaped shell.

Auger

"Auger" means drill, and sea snails often live in these long, thin, twisty shells.

Conch

Large and beautiful sea snail shells with many frills and ridges.

NIGHT-TIME GARDEN TRAIL

All sorts of creatures wake up when it gets dark, from bats and badgers to moths and owls, and, if you're lucky, some will come to your garden. Here are some ways to spot and identify your night-time visitors…

Go out at dusk or dawn, when there's just enough light to see. Be as quiet and still as you can. Nocturnal animals – those that are most active at night – have excellent eyesight, hearing or sense of smell and may easily detect you.

Leaving a light on outside when it's fully dark will attract insects such as moths and spiders looking for a snack. For a good look at flying minibeasts, make a light trap (page 66). Encourage hedgehogs and badgers to visit by leaving out bowls of fresh water. Now and again, especially in cold weather, you can leave out plain kitten biscuits for hedgehogs, or wet cat or dog food for badgers.

61

THE NIGHT SKY

There are all kinds of wonders in the night sky if you know where to look, but it can be difficult to see the stars if you live in an urban area with a lot of bright lights.

Some stars and constellations are only visible in one half of the sky – either the Northern Hemisphere or the Southern Hemisphere – and some can be seen from anywhere. Making sure an adult is with you, find an area as far away from any streetlights as possible to stargaze.

Comet

Comets are huge icy objects flying through space and often contain a lot of rock. They glow in the light of the sun, and have "tails" of gas and dust millions of miles long.

Shooting Star

Shooting stars are not really stars, they're pieces of space rock (meteors) falling to Earth. They are going so fast that the air rushing past them heats them up so that they glow and eventually burn up.

Planets

There are five other planets in our Solar System
that you can see without a telescope – Mercury,
Venus, Mars, Jupiter and Saturn.

Mercury

Venus

Mars

Jupiter

Saturn

SPOTTING STARS

For thousands of years, people have used the stars to find their way. If you can see the stars in the night sky, you can find out which way is north, or south, depending on where you are in the world.

As the year goes on, the stars move around the night sky, turning around us. But some stars don't appear to move much at all, and it's those that we can use to point the right way.

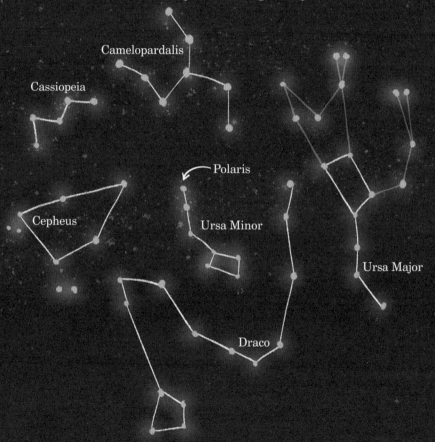

In the Northern Hemisphere, you can see Polaris, the North Star. This star sits almost directly above the North Pole, so if you're facing directly towards it, you're facing north.

In the Southern Hemisphere we cannot see Polaris, so instead we will find south. Look for the constellation called Crux – this is also known as the Southern Cross.

Centaurus

Crux

Carina

Circinus

Musca

Triangulum Australe

Chameleon

Volans

Apus

Mensa

Octans

South Celestial Pole

Pavo

Hydrus

Dorado

Reticulum

Tucana

Eridanus

Now look for the South Celestial Pole. Draw an imaginary line from Crux until you reach the South Celestial Pole. Draw a line vertically down from the South Celestial Pole – you've found the South Pole!

MAKE A LIGHT TRAP

If you want to learn more about nocturnal insects, there's an easy – and fascinating – way to find out.

You will need:

- a clothes line or rope
- an old white sheet
- tent pegs
- a torch
- string
- a clear jar with a lid

1. Choose a dark spot with plenty of trees to set up your light trap up in. Set up your trap in the early evening while there is still some light.

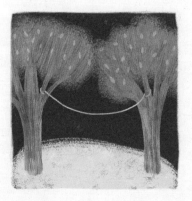

2. Tie a clothes line or rope between two trees and hang a sheet over it.

3. Use tent pegs to fix the sheet to the ground so that it stays still.

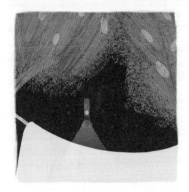

4. Use the string to hang a torch from a tree branch so it dangles over the sheet. Turn it on.

5. When it's dark, the light will attract insects to land on the sheet. Gently place the open jar over an insect, slide the lid under the jar and screw it on.

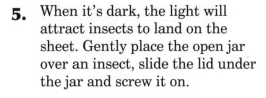

6. When you have finished looking at the insect, carefully let it go.

Here are some of the minibeasts you might see:

☐ mosquitoes   ☐ moths

☐ caddisflies   ☐ beetles

☐ crickets   ☐ hornets

WILDLIFE DETECTIVE

Find out who is visiting your garden at night by making a footprint tunnel. Animals who walk through your tunnel will leave footprints on paper in a special ink (one that is safe for them to touch.) Here's how to make one:

You will need:

- a big piece of cardboard
- strong sticky tape, such as duct tape
- paper
- a little tray or bowl for bait
- some cat or dog food
- vegetable oil
- carbon powder (available from health food shops or online)
- string

1. Fold your cardboard into three to make a triangle, then lay it flat again

2. Use tape to stick the tray or bowl in the centre of the middle section of the cardboard. This is where the bait goes.

3. Stick a piece of paper either side of the bait tray in the middle section.

4. Put strips of tape on either side of the tray, leaving space on the paper for the animals to leave their prints.

5. To make the ink, mix an equal amount of oil and carbon powder. Paint lots of it on to the tape strips.

6. Fill the tray with cat or dog food. Fold the cardboard back into a triangle shape and make holes at the top so you can tie the sides together.

7. Put the tunnel in a quiet, sheltered place outside and check it every day. Very soon you'll see lots of animal tracks!

Here are some of the footprints you might find:

☐ hedgehog

☐ mice

☐ weasel

☐ badger

☐ squirrel

☐ bird

69

NATURE AT HOME

You don't need to go too far from home to see the beauty and wonder of nature – you can find it in your own back garden, or in the green spaces near where you live. Even the smallest garden or park will be filled with life – it's just a matter of looking closely.

There are lots of things you can do to make your home a welcoming place for wildlife. In this section, we will see how to attract and help birds, bees and butterflies, grow flowers and turn them into beautiful art, and even plant huge oak trees!

MINIBEAST SAFARI

Gardens are home to all kinds of tiny creatures, from bugs and beetles to spiders and caterpillars. We call these tiny creatures "minibeasts". Minibeasts are very important: they tidy up dead plants, make the soil better, pollinate trees and flowers, and are an important source of food for all sorts of other animals. Your garden could contain thousands of different kinds of minibeast! Let's get to know some of our tiny friends…

Ladybird

Many ladybirds love to eat aphids (a type of tiny insect) and can eat more than 5,000 a year!

Snail

A snail's body produces slime that helps them move across the ground or to stick in one place.

Spider

There are more than 45,000 species of spider. Many spin sticky webs made of strong silk to catch their prey.

Worm

Worms are covered in many tiny hairs which help them move about. Worms eat soil and plant waste, and by eating and pooing it out they help make your garden soil better!

Social Wasp

Social wasps mainly eat other invertebrates, and sweet, sticky things, such as nectar and fruit juice.

Caterpillar

Caterpillars spend their time eating as many leaves as possible. When they are ready, they form a cocoon or "pupa" and transform into a butterfly or moth.

Slug

Slugs have two pairs of tentacles on their heads which they use to see, smell and taste food, usually plants and fungus.

Butterfly

Butterflies need heat to keep moving, and often rest in a patch of sunlight to warm up before flying away.

Honeybee

Honeybees spend their days buzzing about picking up nectar and moving pollen from flower to flower – this is called pollination and helps plants reproduce.

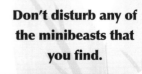

Don't disturb any of the minibeasts that you find.

BIRD-SPOTTING GUIDE

Here are some of the feathered friends you might see in your garden or in woodlands near you. A bird feeder or bird table, with some healthy bird snacks, is a great way to attract them to your garden.

Mistle Thrush

Mistle thrushes may get their name from their love of mistletoe berries – once a berry-laden tree has been found, a mistle thrush will guard the berries fiercely from any other birds.

Great Tit

With black heads, yellow chests and blueish-grey wings and tails, Great Tits like to nest in holes in trees. Sunflower seeds and peanuts will attract them to bird feeders.

Barn Owl

Barn owls hunt at night-time. They use their keen hearing and amazing eyesight to find small animals such as voles and mice, before silently swooping down on them.

Robin

Adult robins are easily identified by their bright red breasts. Both males and females have red breasts, but the males use theirs to warn off rival males.

Starling

Starlings gather in big flocks, and in the winter they will form a "murmuration" – thousands of starlings will fly closely together to keep warm and safe from predators.

Yellow Wagtail

Yellow wagtails hop along the ground hunting for small insects, such as flies and beetles, to eat. They like meadows, farmland and wetlands, and build their nests in long grass and hay in the middle of big fields.

75

GROW AN OAK TREE

Mighty oak trees grow from acorns, and you can grow your own trees in a pot at home. Look after the saplings (young trees) for a few years and then plant them in the ground to grow tall and strong!

Choosing an acorn

You can collect acorns from grown oak trees in the autumn. Pick ones that are green or brown in colour, and without any holes. They should come out of their little caps easily.

You will need:

- 4 acorns (caps removed)
- 15 cm plant pot with drainage holes
- gardening gloves
- trowel
- multi-purpose compost

1. Fill the pot loosely with compost. Leave about a 2.5 cm gap from the top.

2. Make four holes in the compost, evenly spaced around the edge of the pot.

3. Put an acorn in each hole and cover with compost. Water the pot and put it outside.

4. When the roots start creeping out of the drainage holes, move the seedlings to larger pots. Repeat as often as you need to.

Top tip: squirrels, birds and other garden friends may want to steal your freshly planted acorns so you may wish to protect your pot with a net or some mesh.

5. After two or three years, you can plant the saplings in your garden.

MAKE A BEE HOTEL

A bee hotel is just what it sounds like – a safe place for bees to rest and nest. Although we tend to think of bees living in colonies and hives, most species of bees live alone, and making a bee hotel for them is one of the ways you can help these amazing creatures to thrive.

You will need:

- saw
- 10 cm wide untreated wooden plank
- hollow canes, reeds or stems
- drill
- screws
- secateurs
- mirror fixing

1. Saw the wooden plank into four pieces to make a square frame. Drill some guide holes for the screws to fit into and screw the frame together.

2. Add a frame to the back of your wooden square and attach the mirror fixing to it.

3. Cut the canes so they fit the depth of your wooden frame. Make sure each cane is free of blockages.

4. Pack the frame with canes. Once you've found a sunny spot that is sheltered from wind and rain, hammer a nail into the fence and hang up your bee hotel.

5. Bees will plug the ends of the canes with dirt or plant matter, so you can tell when you have visitors.

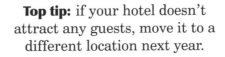

Top tip: if your hotel doesn't attract any guests, move it to a different location next year.

GROWING DAFFODILS

Daffodils are delightful, cheerful spring flowers which you can grow easily. They need little attention and will brighten up your garden for years to come.

You will need:

- gardening gloves
- daffodil bulbs
- pot with drainage holes
- multi-purpose compost
- gardening fork

1. Daffodils grow from bulbs – September or October is the best time to plant them! Fill your pot with compost and use the fork to make sure that the soil is nice and loose.

Safety tip: ask an adult for help when gardening. Wear gloves as daffodils can irritate the skin and always wash your hands after handling daffodil bulbs.

2. Dig holes with the trowel, they should be about 2–3 times the height of the bulbs and at least twice the bulbs' width apart.

3. Put the bulbs in the holes with the thin end pointing up. (You might be able to see some dried roots on the other end of the bulb.)

4. Gently cover the bulbs with peat-free compost and carefully press the soil down.

5. Water the bulbs well after planting. Make sure to water them again if the soil dries out completely.

6. Wait for the spring and enjoy your beautiful new flowers!

MAKE A PRESSED FLOWER PICTURE FRAME

Pick and press flowers to preserve them, and turn them in to a beautiful piece of art to hang on your wall.

You will need:

- flowers
- absorbent paper, such as kitchen roll or newspaper
- heavy books
- a picture frame
- scissors
- art paper or card
- a thin wooden stick, such as a skewer
- PVA glue
- bowl

First pick and press your flowers:

- Flowers are best picked in the morning, on a dry, sunny day, to keep moisture to a minimum.

- Don't pick flowers that are too thick – daisies and pansies work well.

1. Place a piece of absorbent paper inside a heavy book and arrange your flowers on it.

2. Add another piece of absorbent paper on top and close the book carefully, sandwiching the flowers inside.

3. Put something heavy on top of the book and leave it in a cool, dry place for two to three weeks.

When the flowers are nice and dry, it's time to make your flower picture frame:

4. Take the back off the picture frame and cut your art paper or card to the same size.

5. Carefully open your book to reveal your pressed flowers. Be gentle: they are very delicate.

6. Arrange your flowers on the art paper or card until you are happy with their placement.

7. Pour a bit of glue into a bowl. Use a wooden skewer to dab a little glue to the back of each flower.

8. Stick each flower to the paper and let the glue dry for an hour or so.

9. Place the paper into the frame and replace the back. Enjoy your new art!

MAKE A BIRD FEEDER

A bird feeder will attract birds to your garden and provide a useful source of food for them, especially in cold weather.

You will need:

- an apple
- apple corer
- sunflower seeds
- thin sticks or skewers
- scissors
- twine or string

1. Ask an adult to help you remove the apple core. You can do this by using an apple corer.

2. Ask an adult to carefully cut small holes into the outside of the top of the apple. Push sunflower seeds into the holes for the birds to eat.

3. Push one or two sticks or skewers into either side of the apple to make perches for birds visiting your garden.

4. Tie the string or twine around the bottom stick and feed it through the top of the apple.

5. You've made your bird feeder! Tie it to a sturdy tree in your garden and enjoy the sight of the birds that come to visit!

Safety tip: ask an adult to help you use the apple corer.

GARDEN SCAVENGER HUNT

There are all kinds of things to discover in nature – even in your own back garden. How many of these can you and your friends find?

ant

feather

daisy

snail or
slug trail

☐ **cat**

☐ **damselfly**

☐ **moth**

☐ **clover**

☐ **shiny stone**

☐ **hedgehog**

87

MY NATURE DIARY

Use these pages to jot down any interesting
nature observations you've made this year.

Use these pages to sketch any interesting
plants or animals you've seen in nature.

GLOSSARY

atmosphere   The layer of gases that surround Earth, also known as the air.

bacteria   Some of the smallest and simplest living things on the planet. They can only be seen under a microscope but are found everywhere.

canopy   The layer of branches and leaves that spread out at the top of trees in a forest.

colony   A group of animals that live together, often for safety. Many species of birds like to nest together in colonies, and honeybees form colonies called hives.

coniferous   The name given to mostly evergreen plants and trees that produce cone-shaped seed pods, such as pine cones.

deciduous   Trees that lose their leaves when it becomes too cold or dry, or daylength is short – they may shed their leaves in the winter and only grow them back when the weather becomes warmer and brighter.

evaporation   The process through which liquid turns into a gas or vapour.

evergreen   Unlike deciduous trees, evergreen trees do not shed their leaves or needles in winter, and so appear "green" all year round.

fertilizer   Fertilizer is the name given to food for plants. When planting seeds or bulbs, adding fertilizer to the soil will help them grow.

fossil   The remains of plants and animals usually from millions of years ago – dinosaurs, for example – that were covered in mud, sand and silt – and eventually turned to rock.

freshwater   Water that – unlike seawater – is not salty. Most animals and plants prefer either fresh or salty water, but can rarely survive in both.

fungi   A group of living things that are not plants or animals. Mushrooms are the fruiting bodies of some fungi.

gastropod   A group of molluscs that includes slugs and snails. The word "gastropod" means "stomach foot".

gravity   An invisible force that pulls objects towards each other. The gravity of the Earth keeps us – and everything else – from floating away!

habitat   A place where animals, plants or other living things live. Different habitats – whether they are wet, dry, hot, cold or windy – have different things living in them.

hemisphere A hemisphere is half a sphere (ball shape). We call the top and bottom halves of the Earth the Northern and Southern Hemispheres.

lenticels All trees have lenticels, small holes on the surface of a tree's bark. Lenticels help a tree to "breathe".

mollusc A group of animals with soft bodies and no backbones. There are many different kinds of mollusc, from slugs and snails to squid and octopuses.

nectar A sweet, sugary liquid produced by plants, which is an important source of food for many insects.

nocturnal Animals that are awake and active mainly during the night. The opposite of nocturnal is diurnal. Some animals prefer the dawn or dusk, and are called "crepuscular".

nutritious Food that contains plenty of nutrients – the important substances that animals and plants need to grow and be healthy.

pupa The life stage of some insects between larva and adult. Some fully grown caterpillar species makes a cocoon around itself and pupates within it transforming into an adult moth or butterfly.

pollen Many plants reproduce using pollen. Little sticky grains of pollen are produced by the male part of a plant, and must be transferred to the female part for a seed to be formed. Insects can be a very important part of this process, called "pollination".

precipitation Any kind of water falling from the clouds – rain, snow, sleet or hail.

predator An animal which hunts and eats other animals. Cats, spiders, hawks and snakes are all examples of predators.

reproduction The process by which living things make more of themselves – plants produce seeds which grow into more plants.

reptile One of the groups of animals that largely rely on external heat sources to regulate body temperature – they have scales instead of hair or feathers and many reproduce by laying eggs. Crocodiles, alligators, snakes, turtles and lizards are all kinds of reptile.

shoal A big group of fish. Many kinds of fish like to swim together in shoals. This helps keep them safe from predators.

stagnant water Water that stays still and doesn't flow, so it becomes smelly and unhealthy.

vapour When a liquid or solid becomes a gas. When water heats up it becomes vapour and rises into the atmosphere as small droplets of water.

INDEX